Flight

of the

Caged Pelvis

Flight

of the

Caged Pelvis

the
Collected Poems
of

David Calandra

FLIGHT OF THE CAGED PELVIS

iUniverse books may be ordered through booksellers or by contacting:

iUniverse
1663 Liberty Drive
Bloomington, IN 47403
www.iuniverse.com
1-800-Authors (1-800-288-4677)

Because of the dynamic nature of the Internet, any web addresses or links contained in this book may have changed since publication and may no longer be valid. The views expressed in this work are solely those of the author and do not necessarily reflect the views of the publisher, and the publisher hereby disclaims any responsibility for them.

Any people depicted in stock imagery provided by Getty Images are models, and such images are being used for illustrative purposes only.
Certain stock imagery © Getty Images.

ISBN: 978-1-5320-4949-1 (sc)
ISBN: 978-1-5320-4950-7 (e)

Print information available on the last page.

iUniverse rev. date: 06/04/2018

Acknowledgements

For Her
Printed in Celtic Dawn: Volume Four: Oxford, UK. 1991.

Poem Noir
Printed in White Punk Crash: A 'Bad Newz' Papoose:
New York, NY. 1991.

John Dough
Printed in the Clark Street Review: Berthoud, CO. 2006.

Navajo Beauty
Printed in Raccoon: 30/31: Memphis, TN. 1991.
under a pen name, (Aldo Kenyatta)

CONTENTS

Act Two: Comes Zen Goes

Act Three: The Changing of the Mind

Introduction

Origins of 'Flight of the Caged Pelvis'

The poems in this collection were written between (1976-2018), by an aspiring humanitarian who found great enjoyment in creating images with words. Having had no formal training in writing, he found that he could, none the less, write, and under the tutelage of the muses he did so.

Dr. Calandra spent 36 years practicing chiropractic in State College, PA, and having seen thousands of Caged Pelves come through his door, it always reminded him of the title to a poem written by his close friend David Neil Collins, when they were schoolboys in the mid nineteen-sixties. Finding the fixated or "caged" pelvis to be no laughing matter, Dr. Calandra worked tirelessly facilitating the liberation of said pelves. Upon retirement he decided that 'Flight of the Caged Pelvis' would serve as a multi-appropriate title for the collection of poems he had been writing over the years.

Dr. Calandra has committed his remaining years to advancing Caged Pelvis Awareness (CPA), by offering seminars using a variety of results-based modalities, most notably the Pelvic Undulation Exercises®. These are a series of pelvic movements accompanied by the syncopated rhythms of hang drums and tabla—inter-dispersed with the ambient sounds of ocean waves. This is known to generate an ecstatic response often described as a "One with the Universe" experience. Certification as a Caged Pelvis Liberation Instructor (CPLI), is awarded upon completion of the course as well as a membership to the Caged Pelvis Liberation Society (CPLS). As a member of the (CPLS), you will simultaneously be a member of the Caged Pelvis Liberation Front (CPLF), an activist group dedicated to the liberation of human form and function as an important mind-body adjunct to mindfulness and other consciousness exploration techniques.

This collection of poems is presented in three acts with inter-missions at your own choosing.

"One thing I can tell you, is you got to be free."
—John Lennon

ACT I

Dance of the Archetypes

Elephant Man Pushes A Shopping Cart Through The Lobby Of A Bombed Out Building In Downtown Baltimore Only To Discover He Was At The Wrong Address

Needless to say, he'll be needing
                     a new GPS
as soon as he
finds his way through the debris
                 and back onto the street
   to continue his search
              for the proper address
to perform his tricks
           for the amusement of those
      who eagerly await
              his arrival.

The Normal Poem

It didn't start out that way,
the normal poem, that is.
It just sort of evolved from some
dissonant sounds and a cluster
of disparate images.

Soon to take on a life of its own
the normal poem would coalesce
and become a language unto itself,
offering magnificent translations
to be spoken far and near —
for all to hear.

At some point in time, when
the normal poem was first uttered,
everybody was happy.
They would smile and nod to each other
saying, "now that's more like it!"
or, "we'll all sleep better tonight now,
won't we?"

Afterward, as the crowd dispersed
into the street, they talked excitedly
among themselves,
as if the normal poem had just given them
every reason to go home
and wash their windows.

COOKING THE BOOKS

They had given up on get-rich-quick schemes
and decided if they could get a decent education
using a get-smart-fast scheme,
they'd stand a chance of getting a leg up.

So, they headed down to the Book Museum —
(formerly known as the Public Library) and
with a couple of shopping carts,
loaded as many books as they could.

They had heard somewhere, that when you
cooked the books, you could get ahead,
and since it was knowledge they were after
they decided to do just that.
They figured that you could assimilate information
more quickly, if it were served more or less like a soup,
allowing them to accomplish two things
in one fell swoop.
So, they found a giant cauldron, cleaned it up
and filled it with water, herbs, and turnips.
Bringing it to a boil, they began filling it
one book at a time, with salt to taste — stirring occasionally.
When they were sure that the books were cooked,
they sat down at the table, and in-between slurps
discussed what they could do with the riches
they knew would surely be coming their way.

Serenade For A Pit Bull

Once the pit bull had taken his seat in the gallery,
the maestro, baton in hand, turned toward
the orchestra and proceeded to conduct
a most serene piece
for a temperamental beast,
whose only response
was a continuous panting.

Legend has it, that Fredric Chopin
while traveling by train from
Poland to Paris,
met a young aspiring composer
who was deathly afraid of pit bulls.
Upon seeing one he would often develop tremors
that sometimes lasted for weeks, rendering him
incapacitated and only able to think
in Minor keys.

Eventually, the young composer would
get his wits about him and stay awake for days,
composing another masterful piece
that unbeknownst at the time
would someday get airplay.

Chopin, having acquainted himself with
this young talent and after learning of his
problem with pit bulls, decided to offer him
the opening stanzas of a serenade
he had tucked away in his vest pocket,
but only under the condition that
the young composer complete the work
in such a way that it would cure him
of this terrible pit bull affliction.

This was quickly agreed upon, and as the train
roared into the night, loud laughter and barking
could be heard intermittently.

Flashback: Make Love, Not War

I want to kiss your nipples for peace
during a light show
at the Avalon Ballroom.
Traversing time and space, we find ourselves
on the dance floor as the Jefferson Airplane
begins to play, "3/5th's Of A Mile In 10 Seconds".

Strobes of light splashing: white, red, and blue,
delighting our senses and you, smiling,
lower your dress straps.
And I, without hesitation, proceed to kiss
first one, then the other —
my head moving like a metronome
in time with each bounce.
And when the last notes reverberate
from Jorma's guitar
the war that rages a half-world away
comes screeching to a halt—
for just a brief moment.

FLIGHT OF THE CAGED PELVIS (TAKE TWO)

When 'Flight of the Caged Pelvis'
first appeared in print, very few knew
it was destined to become a hit among
libertines and aviation experts alike.
Originally intended to be a one act play,
the choreographer, a stalwart advocate of
artistic temperance, became so ecstatic
she ran off with a band of Trobriand Islanders
who were there for an audition, and the production
was quickly shelved.
When informed of this, the cast and production crew
were disheartened to the point of despondency.

"If it's all for naught, is it not at all?" asked the
make-up artist, stacking her equipment cases.
The stage manager seemed perplexed and deferred
to the production manager, who in turn
asked the orchestra if anyone could speculate as to
the whereabouts of the beloved Winged Pelvis.
They all looked at the empty cage and shook their heads.
A voice rose sheepishly from the string section,
"somewhere in Melanesia, the last I heard,"
said the cellist, giggling.
They all nodded in agreement.

Overwhelmed with emotion, the leading man
walked over to the cage, went in, and pulled
the door closed. "I'm not coming out until I get
a revised copy of the script!" he declared, his jaw
firmly fixed with determination.

The poet-playwright knew he needed to get to work
and rewrite the play as a Mock Epic Poem, with all
the embellishments necessary for a presentation,
not unlike a Wild Incantation.
This took a little longer than he anticipated, and
by the time he returned to the theater, he found
the lead man shriveled on the floor of the cage
like some sort of mummified fruit that had
long ago been hung out to dry.

Meanwhile, worlds away —
the choreographer and her new buddies
were busy building a living shrine
for the beloved Winged Pelvis,
knowing they had finally found
the rightful home
for this glorious creature, who,
only days before,
had been caged and left for dead.

Piano Means "Softly" In Italian

After the fact and before the second coming,
we carry pails of water in silence
up the path to our cabin,
and as we arrive, you turn to me and say,
"piano means "softly" in Italian."

Standing among lattices of wire and wood,
preparing the clay and papier-mache,
we ponder our moves and lay out the tools
and I think about the time you stood
naked in the moonlight, your body wet
with cool, green clay,
telling me for the very first time,
piano means "softly" in Italian.

Though we may suppose that limitless space
can accommodate our reasonable efforts,
these odd figures we form with our hands
are drying as fast as we make them.

Sacred cows, screeching owls, and angels
riding bareback through heaven —
we go on endlessly
with sure hands and steady lines —
with simple, uncomplicated vision,
creating new shapes for image dealers
to peddle beneath street lights
on warm summer nights
in cities we played in as children.

Yes, piano means "softly" in Italian.
And, so we sit — wet clay on our hands
and contemplate how to shape our world,
as the morning sun comes piano
through the window.

FRAGMENTOS

Art is a paradoxical process, on the order of
spontaneous temperance.

Baby dinosaurs find their way to America
and start a revolution in a place called Montana.

As the crow flies, cool breezes blow over
once historical landscapes.

The designs on her skin displayed lunar maps
good enough for a soft landing.

The poets will often illuminate their language
for greater effect in darkened rooms.

I have seen too many gods to become very rich.

I always wanted to read the poems
that my grandfathers never wrote.

Closed minds call it a day.

Deep inside some forgotten musing, a clumsy
con-artist falls through the cracks.

To rest on one's laurels is okay — so long as you
don't make a permanent fixture of it.

Iambic pentameters preclude destiny's hard bargain.

We stroll along the promenade,
as traffic lights regulate the hum of our city.

Poem On A Barn Wall

For David Neil Collins

A poem scribbled on a barn wall
means nothing to the horses, sheep and cows.
In a modern age, pastoral remnants recede
into memory of a family farm with an old barn
and its faded Mail Pouch tobacco sign, along with
some rusted Burma Shave sequence signs
stacked behind bales of hay,
where the horses neigh and chomp.

On the wall beside the barn door, inky scratches
inter-dispersed with carved glyphs
give a translation of how a weird ape
got the notion to turn the world upside down —
creating what we know today as Psycho-earth.
And though it would, in time,
become an Epic poem,
it starts with the mention of
a closet full of midgets, (or what we now call
little people), but it fails to tell us
how many, or what gender.
This is left to the reader's discretion.

Psycho-earth? Well, let's see…
Where did things go wrong?
Psycho-earth wasn't built in a day, or was it?
A talking snake in the second stanza
offers a clue, not to be misconstrued
as a proclamation,
but rather as a hint that maybe
we got it all wrong early on.

Cock-a-doodle-doo!!! Cock-a-doodle-doo!!!
At dawn's first light, the poet awakens
and what comes to mind are a series
of vignettes depicting the trials and tribulations
of Psycho-earth and its lunatic population.
Time traveling back to more idyllic days,
he lounges among the bales of hay,
counting the chickens before they hatch
and tuning his fiddle for the next barn dance.
Soon he will start up the tractor
and head out for the day.
He's got plenty more seeds to sew,
before there'll be time for more Do-Si-Do.

Dancing Lessons

If not for the primitive willingness
Of tribal ritual dancers
Moving between light and darkness!
Pounding the earth with rhythm!
Barefoot, trimmed in feathers!
Loins wrapped in animal skin!
Planetary vegetable masks!
Simultaneous erectus!
With visions of undulating coitus!
Polarized against a cool backdrop
Of ancestral shadows —

We would never have learned to
Square Dance, to Tango, or to Twist.

No Clocks, No Rules, No Clothes

Above in the nooks and crannies
of an old condemned building
pigeons huddle and coo.
Below in a doorway, amidst piles
of newspaper and debris,
a woman sleeps in a box.

Morning glories grow
wildly nearby.

And in the first light of dawn, as
the interwoven fabric of time
finally tears —
we find ourselves in a garden of
planetary vegetables and forbidden fruit.

There are no clocks, no rules, no clothes.

Mannahatta: Y Two K

In the very early morning,
when the first sounds of birdsong
begin to fill the air,
I take a walk through the park
at Tompkin's Square — where
visions of midnight angels
dissolve in the brightening sky.

And as I walk, a flock of pigeons
part before me, and I see they are
birds of a feather. But who are we,
collectively, if not humans alone
with our thoughts?

Now, the old gray-bearded bards
might disagree, but they haven't been
seen in these parts
since the last turn of the century
though it seems like yesterday
when the Hudson and the Harlem
and the East Rivers flowed
unfettered
and flourished with fishes,
with furry little animals
burrowing on their banks.
Surely, it was here that the graybeards
had gathered to chat and to speak
their mindful art.

O' Mannahatta:
your halcyon days are the stuff
from whence Western dreams
once were made.
And who's to say what price we pay
for living each and every day, among
the tall buildings, the traffic, the trains,
— going uptown, going downtown,
from Columbia to Chinatown —
from the Westside to the Eastside,
in a mad rush just to get inside
and off the crowded streets that clamor
like crazy around every corner!

And, so I sit on a bench in this park
watching the sun splash its gold
through the grey —
and I'm thinking of you,
O' Mannahatta:
a new century is dawning
on this New Year's Day.

Gargoyles

All things come to rest
As gargoyles of wisdom
Ponder upon the stone
Of their features
Smooth, yet jagged
Not unlike Sylvia Plath's
Moribund hooks —
Clustered together
As metaphors in marble
Contrived and grotesque
Memories in stone
Gothic and macabre
Guardians of the Palace:
A Council of Demons frozen in time.

Fragmentos

God created the buttocks
so you'd have a place to sit down.

The thing is: everything returns to
shimmering, cosmic, vibrations of bliss.

Scientific investigation
rarely leaves room for coddling.

There are limitations of matter — mostly the grey.

People, primitive at first, soon became
handy enough to destroy everything around them.

Hurt feelings left unresolved,
begin to rain gently
down another cold shoulder.

Lessons from the one-legged dominatrix
are not to be taken lightly.

Whoever upsets the apple cart
better know how to make applesauce.

The silence between notes increases
until the fat lady falls
through the floorboards.

There are fables too old to be told,
for ears too young to hear.

JAMES DOUGLAS MORRISON

Beside the grave of James Douglas Morrison,
she began to sing a few verses from the song
he had given to her, just days before he passed away.
First, she sang in English, then she sang in French.
Either way, the influence of Mallarme, could be
clearly discerned
like a wild child once again reborn
to the cool morning's struggle.

The cemetery at Pere Lachaise is the final
resting place for the singer-poet who used up
all of his time in only twenty-seven years.
And although this brought tears to the eyes
of she who loved him madly —
one eye teared joy
while the other teared sorrow —
knowing there would never be another tomorrow
to touch the face of her beautiful friend,
her Dionysian lover, who would find no sanctuary
in the City of Light,
having woefully lost his way.

Black Jack Boots

The murder of Federico Garcia Lorca
was not so different from the murder
of those standing on either side
of him at the time.

When the smoke cleared, a pile of bodies
lie twitching and moaning,
blood splattered,
soaked in spirit, as though
lily of the valley
beside black jack boots
would make still-life appear
even more still.

But could the voice of a poet
speak for the lot?

Apparently not.

Principles Of Netting

Lessons learned are placed in order
And labeled as coded mantra.
Fishnets, butterfly nets, tennis nets,
Hair nets, safety nets, internets —
All woven webs looking for a catch.

Absurd compulsions notwithstanding,
The firmament brightens with yet another day.
Particular sequences of events, once sequestered
Are now on open display.

I dream of a laughing Buddha
As an eternal presence in
The everlasting motor of late-night television.
Like the embodiment of incarnate wisdom,
Buddha simply raises his hand and begins to wave.

By early morning, post-modern people
Take up positions after traveling all night
On highways of disappearing wilderness.
Memories packaged like fruit baskets
Are opened and shared freely.

But the principles of netting come into play here —
Capturing each moment as a token of time:
To be embraced and savored,
To be revered then set free, to rejoin
In perpetuity, with love everlasting.

OLD GREEN, OVERSTUFFED CHAIR

In a room where there is no furniture,
sunlight streams upon the wooden floorboards
and the door to an adjoining room is ajar.
Between these rooms is an alcove,
where an old green, overstuffed chair
sits covered in cobwebs and stardust.

In the next room, a still-life painting
hangs upside down —
and the way the light reflects
upon the objects in this painting
corresponds exactly
to the way the light configures
upon the wooden floorboards
in the room
where there is
no furniture.

At this synchronous moment, while sitting
in the old green, overstuffed chair —
you can consider the difference a day makes,
as dancing light forms a cognitive mirror
reflecting a face that wears no mask.

Seating Arrangements

When one takes a seat, is it not the result
of leaving one's feet,
purposely or otherwise?
Is the relationship between
gravity and metaphysics
simply a matter of time
as Einstein would have us believe?

Consider this:
How many times have you asked a seated person
if the unoccupied seat next to them was occupied?
"Is anyone sitting there?" you ask, inviting yourself
to the empty seat.
And when they respond, "I don't see anyone, do you?"
— doesn't that change your conceptual framework
in regard to pre-existence?

Now, on the other hand, if the seat is "saved",
does that mean it is pre-occupied?
Is pre-occupation necessarily a prelude to occupation?
What if the person for whom the seat is saved,
doesn't show up?
That seat goes unoccupied.
Doesn't that change your mind about the possibilities
of post-existence? Unfulfilled expectations?
If not, it should.

There is general agreement, that in times of war,
an occupational force will stay only as long as there is food.
However, in peacetime,
if one is asked their occupation and they happen
to work on an assembly line manufacturing brassieres,
does that make them a Mammary Support Specialist?
It depends.

"Make bras — not war!" the shift crews
can be heard to say, when resolving workplace disputes.
They are not given to minutia: they know
there's a job to be done, especially when it comes
to preserving the peace.
They simply take their assigned seats at the bargaining table
and hammer out an agreement:
no ifs, ands, or buts.

So, the next time you find yourself in a dilemma
over seating arrangements
don't forget, things could be worse,
there could be standing room only.

Javelina Morning

Having a good day
in the presence of peccaries
devouring your melons
is nearly impossible
if not for the saving graces
of a second growing season
in the high desert of Arizona.

As a cycle of nature, seeds fall
from javelina jaws
only to be re-planted
under dainty hooves
for tomorrow's fresh bounty.

If you want to reap what you sew,
you must construct a barrier
to mess with the minds of these beasts —
sending them brooding into the bush
where they belong.

Their lingering odor is quickly dispersed
by soft breezes of pinion and sage.
While melons bask in the warm morning sun
the pigs file hurriedly into the gulch.

Javelina morning and have a good day.

FRAGMENTOS

He wrote his memoirs on a three by five card
leaving a space in case
there was something he had forgotten.

Without naked knowledge
there would be no need for blinders.

In the heat of passion, hot pink works just fine.

Luminous faces appear at midnight
to gather their belongings.

Ah, Miami…
The jeweled navel of the Western Hemisphere.

Tongues come out to play, as rose petals
fall to the ground.

After much deliberation, he turned to the fella
next to him and asked, "have you ever been taken
on an alien spacecraft?" The man slowly shook
his head and shrugged, "No, they always tell me
there isn't enough room."

Once hatched there will be no turning back.

Ever notice how pelicans seem to smile
when searching for fishes each nautical mile?

POMGADO

In the deepest recesses of humanity's longing,
lies Pomgado.
Good thing, otherwise there would be no hope.
Let's say you come upon a car accident in the driving rain,
and let's say it's a red Toyota Prius.
You know you've come upon an emergency and you begin
to think about everything you learned growing up.
You know there is no choice but to stop and be a first responder.
To do this, you are going to need plenty of Pomgado.
You slow down and pull over. You call 911 and report
the accident, but you have no idea where you are.
For all you know, you may have entered a parallel universe
and you pass this on to the dispatcher.
You are advised to secure the perimeter, so without a moment
to spare, you slide down an embankment and come to
the crumpled Prius.
It is smoking and making loud crackling noises.
You try to look inside but you can't really make anything out.
You pull open the driver's side door and the person sitting there
is staring straight ahead, blood running down his face and from
his ear. You notice that he is wearing an earring that looks like
a yin-yang symbol.
He puts a cigarette in his mouth and asks you for a light.
You look past the driver and see his passenger. She is grinning
as though she is in a stupor. She's holding a cracked mirror,
but is no longer wearing her wig.
You ask them if they are alright and suggest that they get
out of the car.
Just then you notice tiny angelic beings descending and tending
to the couple as police sirens can be heard in the distance.
Having been relieved of your duty and on your way home,
you begin to feel good about yourself, knowing that Pomgado
will always be there when you need it.

Let's say the next day, some members of the Wambezi tribe
from Southern Kalahari, appear at your door with a package.
They have big smiles on their faces and they begin to coax you
into opening this package in their presence. Not wanting to step
on any toes, which would be easy to do since they are all barefoot,
you begin to open the package.
You hear little scratching noises coming from inside and you
also hear what sound like faint, muffled screams.
You know you are in another awkward situation and once again
you will need plenty of Pomgado.

You open the package and to your surprise
it's the couple from the Prius you had met the day before.
And are they glad to see you!
They climb into your hand and you place them
on a table in the vestibule.
Meanwhile, the Wambezi's begin slapping their chests
and making loud clicking noises with their mouths.
You take this to mean that it's time to part with
the goat meat and chickens you had stored in the freezer.
You retrieve the meat and put it in a sack along with
some canned goods and a six-pack of Coors light beer.
The Wambezi's are very excited and bow to you repeatedly
as they leave your premises.
You close the door and turn to your little friends —
but they have disappeared.
They did not want to be held accountable for any imposition.
You see them climbing out an opened window,
closing it behind them as they go.
You shake your head in disbelief and once again
begin to feel that warm, reassuring glow, letting you know
that having plenty of Pomgado makes all the difference
in the world.

Some Poems (No. 1)

Some poems are like bones on the beach
washed up on shore with the tide,
glistening white, they shine in the sand
as seabirds walk circles around them.

WILLIAM TELLING IT

And then there was William telling it —
feet set firm beneath swift currents
body ablaze
in cadmium red, but with no head,
instead, an apple suspended in air,
ripe, but with no worms.

At sunrise an archer takes aim
and shoots an arrow
striking a sequence of apples —
sending seeds to germinate,
unnoticed.

An empty chair sits in an open meadow
where bright blood
drop by drop,
feeds the fresh morning.

Two eyes gaze from an opening
in fields of buttercup.

Wispy clouds float slowly above treetops
as a birdlike creature — but with no wings,
walks slowly to the border
and finding no frame,
disappears into the wilderness.

From a painting by the author: oil on canvas, 1974.

Finishing Touches

I once thought about painting a still-life
of a top hat on a table, surrounded by bones:
a clavicle, a fibula. a scapula, a tibia,
a nice tablecloth, and perhaps
a bowl of cherries or kumquats.

But instead I settled for a portrait of Kate,
who could pose in deep thought like no other.

Sometimes she would think about silly things,
like teaching ballroom dancing to Hell's Angels,
or playing a squeezebox in a jammed packed
subway car.

Sometimes she would imagine herself
strolling down Main Street
wearing an assortment of accoutrements,
such as a ruby-studded gun belt,
or a necklace of animal fetishes,
or shoes that could take her back to Kansas
at a moment's notice.

Sometimes she would gather her thoughts
and give them priorities, forming a mandala
of sorts, with the deepest thoughts in the center.
Sometimes she would consider algorithms
and their relationship to existentialism.
Sometimes she could hear music using her
Third Ear, much in the way Peruvian shamans
use their Third Eye in Ayahuasca ceremonies.

Sometimes she would tilt her head to the left,
sometimes to the right, blinking rapidly, then
returning to center with a positional attitude
that made her presence all the more endearing.
Breathing gently, she would imagine Kundalini
as the source of all things that stand erect.
Conversely, she considered gravity as the cause
of all things at rest.

In between strokes, she would
often suggest we revisit the time
when love was spoken
with tongues untwisted.
I would remind her that she had not
yet skipped a beat
when it came to showing
her womanly prowess.

Sometimes she would grow restless
and practice her pouting,
in case she ever had reason to brood.
But, mostly she would just sit there —
in perfect stillness, as if she were a statue
of none other than herself.

When the session ended, she would come
take a look, and taking a brush
she would add a stroke,
always eager to render the finishing touches.

MENAGE A TROIS

The sentimental cubist and the cynical realist
decided to leave some canvas behind
for their friend, the surrealist,
who was sure to come stumbling
into the studio
sometime in the wee hours,
searching for meaning in the juxtaposition
of certain distorted relationships.

"If we stick together, we won't come apart!"
said the cubist closing the door.
"If we do come apart, we can always
tele-communicate," replied the realist,
completely aware that surrealism
often leads to estrangement.

Keeping this in mind, they went off
into the night
after exchanging identities,
less they forget
their whereabouts.

As Luck Would Have It

She, with lips parted
Tongue alluring, awaits a stroke
Of luck to strike
Abruptly
Without warning
Without reservation, as another
Orgasmic memory emerges
From a long ago
Star-pod.

LONG AND HARD

Sometimes you have to look
long and hard
to see the true meaning
of an object at hand. And
upon closer exam you'll begin
to notice, that which at first
is not apparent.
But, as you look
long and hard,
it all begins to make sense.
And you can rest assured
knowing full well
the importance of looking
long and hard.
Long and hard, long and hard,
it all begins to make sense.
And you can rest assured
knowing full well
the true meaning
of an object at hand.

FRAGMENTOS

A woman knows the value of a gentleman
and she looks for him when she enters a room.

If I were a notebook and you were a pen,
how would you describe yourself to me?

Inside your narrow corridor, I somehow
feel connected to wide open spaces.

We duck into a little café, vowing
not to re-emerge
until we're good and ready.

Nude beaches appear on the horizon.

It's as simple as this: start each day
as though you're going to transfigure
yourself into a better person.

The 'Melodramatics' have taken
the stage, to play some short numbers
for quick dance steps
at the Annual Little People's Convention.

When Molly Incognito revealed herself,
no one seemed to notice.

It is better to forget some things
than to remember others.

TREE

The tree is a leafy spirit,
sentient and sublime.
Deep are its roots,
stirring, searching.
Strong is its trunk,
a pillar amongst pillars.
Sturdy are the limbs,
wild are the branches,
laughing are the leaves.

Go figure.

Right In The Kisser

The other day I walked up to
the President of the United States
and threw a pie in his face.
You're probably wondering how
I'm still here telling you about this
and not languishing in some dungeon
in the basement of the White House.
Well, it's like this:
it was around lunchtime
and the President had just finished
delivering an address,
not unlike how one might deliver,
say, birthday balloons.
When he went to leave the podium
I appeared suddenly, seemingly
out of nowhere, with my very own version
of pie in the sky.
After making my delivery, right in the kisser,
the secret service agents (needing
to make up for lost time),
moved in quickly to secure me.

Always willing to make reparations,
I invited them out to lunch.
Looking at each other, they began to shrug
and nod their heads, saying, "what the heck?"
So, we headed down to Fugazzi's Cafe
to get some food and drink
and watch re-runs of the President
wiping lemon meringue pie off his face
as he reassured a nervous nation
that even the head honcho can take a little
pie in the face, now and again.

CONCRETE

A tone poem with embellished prose pieces
will often present an idyllic version of
a severed reality.

Arpeggios aside, let us begin:

Sky blue, birds flew —
o'er seas of concrete
where sidewalks crack
with sprouted seed
suggesting things like:
nature grows
in spontaneous silence,
or, we get more clear
with occasional thunder,
or, with no stone left unturned
the search party returns empty handed
and in complete agreement
that lost verses are best found
by chance.

Is it any wonder that Achilles
fell head over heels
into the abyss of mortality?
Is it any wonder that we insist
on freedom
for burqa-clad goddesses
chained to oblivion
by an ill-conceived notion?

Houdini couldn't figure it out, but he tried.

Think about it: a mind trained to simply comply,
will catch only a glimmer of life's grandest proposal.

But, wait!
There's an easy transition here:

More concrete poured fresh and smooth —
soon to be filled with footprints and handprints;
etched with words like: Fuck, or Peace, or
Patty Loves Tommy —
with symbols of anarchy, or simple directives
like, 'Go This Way'— or, 'Watch Your Back!'

Once, well inscribed, it begins to take shape,
firming up for its special place in time.
And although it began as a smooth surface,
just an ordinary stretch of grey —
a tone poem with embellished prose pieces
will always provide a fanciful interlude
on the path of no return.

Encore

Just when you thought it was safe
to be dead,
they come around with flashlights
and a list with your name on it.
They want to know if you're willing
to make an appearance
in a late-night movie
as an apparition
who haunts a nice family
in a middle-class bedroom community.

You respectfully decline, but they
won't take "no" for an answer.
So, you go with them to a place
called Livingston
and take up residence
in a modest split-level home,
only to find the nice family
wasn't so nice after all.
This caused great consternation
among the film crew — allowing you
to slip out the door and return to
the blessed anonymity
you so rightfully deserve.

Fragmentos

The Jack in Kerouac, is not the same
as a jack-of-all trades —
which is why Neal Cassady
always went along for the ride.

Common courtesy lies crumpled in a corner,
ham-strung and hog-tied.

Sometimes I feel like a Cyclops
wearing an eye-patch.

Iguanas cry out in the moonless night
as our signal to begin the long journey home.

"Waiter! Please bring some pink bananas
for the gorilla of my dreams!"

He thinks this class is physics, but he
couldn't remember what day it was.

She prefers to think of neutrinos as a kind of fruit
invented somewhere near Fresno.

If existence is controlled chaos,
why struggle to give up the struggle?

Why the cape?

Why do hog-washers like to spread bullshit?

A Haven For Clowns

Back before the days of Babylon,
the clowns waited till midnight
before showing their faces.
These days, you can see them anywhere,
any time, day or night.
Some folks find clowns to be creepy,
some find them funny, but when
you ask a clown, "what gives?"
they'll usually just scratch their head
and honk that little horn
they have fastened to their belt.
How you interpret this depends upon
how well acclimated you have become
to polite society.

If you have been properly schooled,
you will, of course, laugh,
but if you are a rugged individualist,
or a wayward miscreant,
you will most likely remain silent,
barely cracking a smile — then give
a little shrug and walk away.

Clowns come in all shapes and sizes, but
they all have one thing in common —
an unbridled urgency to clown around
and poke fun.
Some clowns have small cars.
Some clowns have big feet.
Most are known to wreak havoc on pillow cases.
Most clowns are men.
It's been said, it is unbecoming for a woman
to appear as a clown
though some will do it anyway.

The next time you come face to face
with a clown, just remember,
beneath the make-up lies a tormented soul,
or a friend of a friend, or a semi-retired lion tamer
who lost an arm and a leg, bossing big cats around.
No matter.
A clown will always command your attention
and give you every reason to laugh,
or to sneer.

Foxy

Whoever told you there's
no place to hide
is trying to pull the wool
over your eyes.
There's plenty, believe me.
You just have to know the way
of the fox —
which is not to say
you won't get
out-foxed
somewhere along the line
at some point in time.

Look at what happened to Che,
down Bolivia way.

But if you're a foxy lady,
or for that matter, a foxy man,
and you know the terrain
like the back of your hand,
you can out-maneuver
the slobbering hounds
with your cunning ways —
and your leaps and bounds.

Is That You, Garcia?

Armed with a search warrant, police obtained
a sample of Garcia's blood.
Armed with a search warrant, police obtained
an EEG reading of Garcia's brain.
Armed with a search warrant, police kicked
the shit out of Garcia and had IT analyzed.
But that was not enough.

Armed with a search warrant, police wanted
to know Garcia's whereabouts from day one.
They wanted to know what he was doing tomorrow
and the day after that.
They wanted to know if Garcia was really Garcia,
or just another homeboy with
no place left to call home.

And wouldn't you know, Garcia would not cooperate;
he didn't believe in a compelling state interest.
Why should he?
He was in a witness protection program.

GOT A LIGHT?

The scatterbrain is busy making
scrambled eggs, while her lover
lounges in the tub listening to
'The Crazy World of Arthur Brown',
and daydreaming about civilization as
a conceptual nightmare, invented by Lucinda
his beloved dog.

The Dogon tribe in Africa
made famous the dog star Sirius,
but Lucinda made Planet Earth infamous —
crop circles notwithstanding.

Bathe yourself in fire?
No way!
Sectarian pyramids line the landscape;
the sun sets never to return.

THE GOLDEN CALF

As I begin the long journey home,
I carry across my shoulders the golden
calf of Isis.
And on my journey, I walk the back alleys
through Newark's morning mist:
to see dogs humping under cloudy skies
with an occasional burst
of sunlight upon scattered trash
and broken glass
with tires half-submerged in mud puddles
glossed with oil and a couple of
tadpoles destined to become mutant frogs.

Then, down Frelinghuysen Avenue
and into Elizabeth — to see daffodils
plowed under by bulldozers
clearing away the debris from
the demolished Burry Biscuit factory.
I make note of this, then head left
onto North, to roam the landscape
in search of spring chickens
that just got up and walked away.

Anyway, when the kids came out to play
in streets full of potholes and spray-paint,
they ask to feed the golden calf
some of their Cracker Jacks and Kool-aid.
I agree to this in exchange
for the prize inside the box.

Upon finally reaching my destination,
I place the golden calf on a Pedestal of Peace.
Then, slowly opening my prize,
I find a plastic Eye of Horus, winking at me,
as I turn it ever so slightly.
This tells me it's time for quiet repose
and I rest my head in the lap of Hathor.

Some Poems (No. 2)

Some poems are like snakes in the grass:
slithering, belly-down, smooth.
With tongue in the air, they can go anywhere
and that's what they usually do.

FRAGMENTOS

The artist returns to bright pigmentation
just before the lights go out.

The muses are all in bed with me
and they're creating a ruckus!

Faces reflected in a pond look attentive.

The actors tip-toe across a darkened stage
sensing danger coming from the empty seats.

Once you have an encounter with a UFO,
visitation rights take on new meaning.

Keep your mask handy; one never knows
what a warthog will do in a fire fight.

If you enjoy tongue in cheek, the next time
you're in Paris, give it a try.

Small talk becomes very small talk
until it is merely a murmur.

What is education, if not war on stupidity?

His psychedelic banjo burst into flames
causing the Fire Marshall to lose his temper.

She put the flute to her lips.

The lost and found will always remain
more lost than found.

Pink Lady

Julia, of the romantic high blue church music,
it's what you call, 'Little House on the Prairie' music,
not one for the heinous low rumble of red-hot music,
those wretched red-hot sounds that jangle the nerves
leaving you quivering deliriously.
Life is secure in a 'Strawberry Shortcake' sleeping bag
complete with matching umbrella.

Julia, your sister called to say you are nuts
and to send you back out to Palm Springs
where she can cool you down
with nice turquoise threads —
and some soft sounds, from the High Blue Church.

She said to tell you Tim Leary is dead,
and that his brain has been frozen
somewhere in Scottsdale—
that it's now safe to return
and give up your search
for that 'Little House on the Prairie'.

UNCLE KNUCKLEHEAD

I couldn't help but notice
Uncle Knucklehead standing by
the water-cooler conversing with
invisible entities.
No one really knows what goes on
inside his head, but lately he's been
seen knocking on it, and saying things like,
"who's there?" or, "hello, is anybody home?"

Uncle Knucklehead, always the practical joker
likes to pull pranks everyday —
even if it means pulling one on himself
which he has been known to do.

Uncle Knucklehead never sleeps.
In fact, no one has ever seen his bed,
and when asked, he simply says,
"don't need one… did you ever see yourself
asleep in a dream?"

Uncle Knucklehead laughs at the drop of a hat,
so the townsfolk hold on tight to their hats
whenever he comes around.
But on a windy day —
watch out!

Uncle Knucklehead will often disappear
sometimes for months, claiming he
travels with the circus.
But others say they heard him
telling old Mrs. Huckabee
the day before she passed away,
how flying saucers would come pick him up
whenever they needed an Ambassador;
that he was the best they ever saw
and they really liked his availability.

Janet Eats Grasshoppers

Getting past the wings is the easy part,
then you come to the head with those
beady little eyes, "bug-eyes" we'd call 'em.
Then there's that brown, tarry substance
coming from their mouth, as if
they've been chewing tobacco all day.
And then there's those jagged little legs,
those awful jagged little legs. No matter.
Janet never felt quite at home with
Dairy Queens, or Burger Kings.
No, her omnivorous instincts were quite satisfied
by those remarkable creatures flying around
out back. Just a hop, skip, and jump —
she could be there, her hands quick to grasp —
Crunch!
And just then a signal would go off in her brain
that the whole world was right,
that her earliest dreams just might come true,
and that low-calorie snacks could be fun and easy.

ABRAHADABRA

"My head was mashed into wood pulp,
thereon the Daily Newspaper was printed."
                    Aleister Crowley

In modern times the printed word
grows quaint among the artifacts.
A long table offers a collection of handbills
arranged in such a way, as to make a colossal display
appear short and to the point.
News of a sphinx spotted walking the streets
of Palermo, spread quickly — but not fast enough
for the authorities seeking retribution
for the shenanigans witnessed
at the Abbey of Thelema.

Abrahadabra

Frater Perdurabo rode backwards on an ass
to catch a last glimpse of his beloved Laylah.
Perhaps the blue-lidded daughter of sunset
would practice a bit of swift green magick
to quicken her way, down the beaten path.
A shrill hawk's cry pierced the coming of darkness
as Perdurabo turns to face the night's long journey.

Abrahadabra

In Hastings, the dank morning found a solitary donkey
standing at the bedside of a well-worn Magus.
The nurse, having entered the room, saw nothing strange.
She set the tea tray in its normal place, took a pulse
and whispered, "you have a visitor, Mr. Crowley."
The Magus opened one eye and upon seeing the beast,
put an index finger to his head and pulled the trigger.

Abrahadabra

Spare Change

Tin cup in hand filled to the brim
with the heads of dead presidents
enough to fill a gallery,
or buy a couple tacos,
or some Wild Irish Rose, or perhaps
a pair of trousers
with really deep pockets.

Breakfast With Satan

"No one has ever written, painted, sculpted, built,
or invented, except literally to get out of hell."

Antonin Artaud

Breakfast with Satan is not
by any stretch of the imagination,
anything like having tea with Jesus.
The black satin tablecloth and napkins
do nothing for the burnt biscuits and dark blue coffee.
As one might expect, there is an absence of fruit
and a conspicuous presence of pig knuckles.
"Fruit is for wimps," Satan explains with a brush of
his hand, "what's up for grabs, is up for grabs,
so you better have yourself a good breakfast."
"Are buns up for grabs?" I think to myself,
watching the waitress loading some onto a tray.
As she passes, I grab one only to find it is rubbery
and squeaks like a dog's toy.
"Some devil's food," I muttered.
Satan is not amused by this, and after staring at me intently
for what seemed an eternity, he finally spoke,
"Have you ever had a donkey sit on your face?"
"No, not that I recall," I responded, taking a quick sip of coffee.
"Oh, believe me, you would remember," he retorted,
clearly agitated that I was amused by his question.
Pausing to fold his hands like the kindly fallen angel
he fancies himself to be, he continued,
"Don't you know that the best way to prepare yourself for death
is to have a donkey sit on your face?"
"Never heard that one before," I assured him, taking a
bite from the burnt biscuit that lie before me.
"Well, now you know. And believe me, there is no greater darkness!"
I pondered over this for a moment and decided
I could use a breath of fresh air.
Excusing myself, I went outside and hailed a cab.
"Where to?" asked the driver. "Hell's Kitchen — right away,
I hear they have a heck of a buffet!"

ERNIE AND DINAH

I watched as Tennessee Ernie Ford
licked chocolate mousse
off the face
of Dinah Shore
who lie sprawled and seemingly
stupefied on the floor
in the lobby
of the Waldorf Astoria, at four
in the morning.

Having envisioned the world
from a different place in time,
I assumed that what I saw was
etiquette about to become extinct,
were it not for the quick thinking
of the Concierge who
ordered the grounds crew
to roll up the floor.

The sun is rising in the West, and I can't
find my trousers anywhere!

Backstage?
Same thing.

When in Atlantis, do as the antediluvians.

Compel, repel, dispel, expel, propel —
so many pels, so little time.

Often the pauses are as important as the tone.

There is no greater immorality than brutality.

We are who we have become.

The lovers linger in silence,
beneath the dark cover of night.

As saxophone players blow sacred jazz hymns,
— she channels Alice Coltrane.

The birds know something we don't know.

Once the serpent sealed our fate,
we quickly learned the meaning of molting.

I'm moving to the Golan Heights;
I've had enough of this shit.

Realism devoid of magnificence
is like a hitchhiker with no arms.

"Between two evils, I always pick the one I never tried before."

—Mae West

ACT II

Come Zen Goes

BLOW

Why do people blow?
Do they feel obligated to do so?
Bubbles, birthday candles, kisses
blown through pursed lips
through thin air —
as an earnest exhalation
rarely missing the mark.

Blow up, blow out, blown away —
blow your horn, blow your mind,
blow me off, blow me down —
or if you happen to be at a ball game
you might even see a blown save.

Everything gets blown… in good time.

Fugs In A Barn

Fugs in a barn
With Swinburne in the rafters!

Blake was there too, counting the sheep.
And Ed knew the muse would cry the blues
If a dirty old man flashed Little Bo Peep.

Fugs in a barn
With Swinburne in the rafters!

Keats was there too, checking out the chicks.
And Tuli's tees would surely seize the day
When baskets of love turned their tricks.

Fugs in a barn
With Swinburne in the rafters!

Belushi was there, asleep in the hay.
And what had become of this Little Boy Blue?
Only the beloved Slum Goddess can say.

Fugs in a barn
With Swinburne down from the rafters!

To lead a sweet chorus in, "Wide, Wide River"
Causing the barnyard banshees to quiver,
On this cool August night in Woodstock.

Woodstock, NY 1988.

Say, Fay

Do you remember when
we spied some red lobelia
down by the river bank
where Brahma bulls
slowly appeared to us
through the morning mist?
I remember, it was my 30th
birthday and the Krishna's
placed a garland of lotus flowers
over my head
making me feel like a Mahatma
just for a day.

A Visit To Nowhere Zen New Jersey

Allen,

Newark's bleak furnished room is still there
after all these years,
as mystified humans knock on opportunity's door.
And when the door opens there is a rarified air,
some say it's breathtaking, others don't seem to notice.

Alphabet City always knew of your whereabouts
and when you would appear beneath streetlights
just before dawn, you could sometimes hear voices
saying, "Look, there goes the poet, he has spoken
great truths far and near, but he lives right here
among the rubble of the American dream!
He is truly our very own!"

Across the Hudson, in Nowhere Zen New Jersey,
the Passaic river grimaces in pain. No need to
offer condolences, the fish are no longer biting.
And what about Paterson?
And what about Atlantic City?
And don't forget Camden!
Which direction doth thou beard point?
What peaches and what penumbras?
Hackensack! Paramus! Tranquility!
Goldfinches in Rutherford
delight the morning sky.

John Dough

They found him beneath a pile
Of nickels and dimes
Stiff as a board with eyes wide open.
The coroner concluded he had been
Dead for days, but the cause of death
Remained a mystery.

Was he crushed to death?
Did he suffocate?
Or did he simply die of fright?
Was it homicide? Was it suicide?
Or was it some form of genocide?
The coroner had plenty of things to sort out,
But heck, if he didn't do it, who would?

Knowing he was nearly clueless,
The coroner began by consulting
A psychic who lived as a subterranean
In the middle of a nearby forest.
Being available only by
Telepathic communication
The psychic could be on any case
With lightning speed if necessary.

In this case, there was plenty of time,
So the coroner sent slow, telepathic messages
Co-mingled with soft forest breezes,
Further decreasing any need for urgency.
This would afford him the opportunity
To attend a banquet in honor of his girlfriend
Ramona, the renowned raconteur.

Later that day,
When the psychic picked up his messages,
He determined instantly that the subject
Whose name, as it turns out,
Was John Dough,
Had been nickeled and dimed to death
By federal agents, and that it was, in fact,
A mercy killing.

The Girl Next Door

Beneath the bright star,
beside the dull planet —
she runs with wild abandonment
kicking up her heels
and cracking the air with laughter.

Disappearing from view,
she reappears like a diamond
in the eye of her beholder
who marvels in awe.

She imagines losing herself in space,
but having such a presence
she finds this impossible.
So, she settles for an occasional
flight of fantasy, returning only
to maintain her composure.

Little by little, she exposes
her left breast. She does not
believe in taboos.

Sure, she is the girl next door
and she will always remind you
that the neighborhood is her oyster.

FRAGMENTOS

The magician's tricks went unnoticed.

She told me she was raised by hippies
which is why she was so adventurous.
I took this to mean she was headed for
the coast and would leave behind only trails.

He speaks of love only because it becomes him.

When Miss Texas was asked to describe
her ideal man, she gave a big smile and replied,
"Not too big and not too small, not too wide
and not too tall."

He offered lessons in insouciance,
for those who were anxious to learn.

Everything gets put on hold
when it's twilight savings time.

He wanted to lick some toads,
but he couldn't find a small enough paddle.

The day is long as it is wide.

Not to be dissuaded, he proceeded to study the manuals,
taking breaks only to tinker with abstract realism
as a possible route of escape.

Uncle Shadow's Garden

In Uncle Shadow's garden
the pods nod in the mid-day sun
quietly discussing the latest news
from the *Vegetable Times Review,*
Above, a dove
coos
in shades of soft blue,
as butterflies move the still air.
Like tiny fluttering clouds with eyes
they make the day come alive.

Beside the trough the watering can glistens
as Uncle Shadow sits and reflects.
In August, the tomatoes will burst into flames,
but first the peas will do as they please.
And when the garden is awash with squash,
Uncle Shadow will motion to his beloved
to ready a pot for some vegetable stew.

Abruzzo Bird

I give to my father everything that is Italian,
because he is Italian and he likes it that way.
Son of immigrants from an Abruzzo bird-tribe,
transplants into the Allegheny plateau —
Altoona, Pennsylvania.

Railroads that go places will need
plenty of precision. All aboard!
— there are myths in the making
and soot everywhere!
So much for safe haven
on the other side of the tracks.

Whistles, metal brakes screeching —
bells clanging, engines chugging, then fading
into another long night.
Boxcars and more boxcars — painted bright
blue, and bright yellow, and dull brown,
carrying cargo bound for faraway places:
Chicago, St. Louis, San Francisco, Santa Fe.

Soon the kids will grow and leave this place,
going along for the journey, just like the cargo —
to supply the demand of a vast and wild land.

And so, I give to my father everything that is Italian,
because he remembers what it's like
to speak a native tongue
and to transmute the impossible
into a Western religion.

LEVITICUS

Leviticus had always lived in the Bronx,
then one day he left his body
and took a job driving a bus
in downtown Bangkok.
His passengers were not impressed.
So, he left the bus in the middle of an intersection
causing a riot that spilled over into Cambodia.
It was here he decided to take up residence
as an expatriate and troublemaker.

Mistaken Identity

If you look closely you can see them
ruminating in the shadows
just beyond life, not far from
where you are now sitting.
Be still and listen; they will soon
make their presence known.

The dead are dying to be heard
and they'll do anything
just to get in a word.
They've been around the block
so they know quite well
why the hairs on your head
are all numbered.

No, it's not a figment of anyone's
imagination
to hear the hubbub
of their elaborate enumeration,
in fact, it happens all the time.
Whether you're a friend, a Roman,
or you just prefer country living,
the day will come to lend them your ear.

Now, far above the din
of their knowledgeable discourse,
where wisdom melds to gold —
after all is said and done,
a consensus emerges and is spoken as such:

"To be, or not to be — means nothing,
when you assume a mistaken identity."

Some Poems (No. 3)

Some poems are like couples in love,
rocking and rolling all night;
when they fall out of bed
and land on their head
somehow it doesn't seem right.

Fragmentos

In between a parade of clouds, we spot
the imaginary presence of clowns.

He who writes it down best,
sees her standing in the doorway.

Unsanctioned sacrifices to save the deviants
caused great consternation among the naysayers.

Her ass was plump, not unlike a ripe plum
and that's all I remember.

Wilhelm Reich was right about a lot of things
and wrong about a few.

Sharing is caring and caring is sharing,
however way you want to break it down.

Some go in hair shirts for Zen reasons,
while others go with no shirt for no reason.

The power of trust and faith
is an important consideration
when it's time to go and not return.

As Mammon speaks, the Oligarchs listen.

This planet is not a very good place to raise kids.

There is consciousness beyond brain, to think
otherwise is rather presumptuous.

DISCREET

Frank Zappa once wrote a song called
"Muffin Man", but he failed to provide
any of his usual embellishments,
leaving them instead to the listener's
own discretion, or indiscretion,
whichever seemed most appropriate,
or inappropriate, depending upon the
listener's predilection for signature changes,
or the lack thereof.
Needless to say, this caused incredible chaos
among bakers and eccentrics alike.

Jessica Gold And Anna Moss

Jessica Gold and Anna Moss lie
inextricably intertwined.
No one could ever pull them apart,
no bindings could they find.
Then one day a snake charmer
showed and began to play real slow —
when Jessica Gold and Anna Moss
suddenly let go!
And walking sprightly, bare-ass naked,
down O'Leary Lane,
Jessica Gold and Anna Moss
would never be the same.

TOE RING

A warrior poet's lament
awakened the heart of she who
believes in curved air.
Incidental dreams replenish the spirit
of he who knows the meaning of tears.
She imagined herself in his boots
walking up the side of a tree
and into a nest of crows.

For a moment, he gazed into her eyes
and said nothing.
Time has no meaning here.
Eternity, condensed into an urge
will always remain silent.

His battle was simply a
blood offering to the muses,
and when this was finally understood,
she immediately offered to lick his wounds.

She suggested that he consider
how his very freedom depended
upon his ability to let go of reason.
He noticed she was wearing a toe ring.
He considered this a sure sign of wisdom
and decided to take her advice.

Now, far from his mind, he began
to chortle, bemused by everything he saw.
She removed her toe ring and placed it
in his hand, closing it gently as she spoke,
"up is down and down is up,
and surely as frogs do croak,
the answers to your questions lie
within the words you spoke."

Not being one to beat around the bush,
he began to beat his poems into ploughshares.
And when he looked up, she was gone.
He knew he'd never see her again
though it be no reason to fret:
he never dreamed he'd find
such equanimity,
with a toe ring for his treasure.

She Means Business

Her suit is not diminished
at thirty-thousand feet,
it is where she can work small wonders.
Consciously, she moves mountains
in the board room, where she's
offered a cigar, which she declines.
The corporate ladder is waxed
with the semen of giants
and tomorrow she will take a vacation
to hike naked in the Galapagos —
cutting deals with a different kind
of creature.
It's what keeps her sharp and ready
for the next merger.

The Obligatarians

The Obligatarians are a tribe within a tribe,
sort of like a culture within a culture,
and although one cannot really say that
they are a subculture, they will often
give that appearance.

The Obligatarians are best known
for their mind reading abilities.
Some claim they even know
what you're going to say
before you say it,
which of course
affords you the opportunity
to save your breath
while in their company.

The Obligatarians never think twice
about giving you a pat on the back
even if you don't deserve one.
They'll always be there, to pat your back,
just to let you know they're around.

The Obligatarians will appear nightly
— if you let them. They serve as a reminder
that it's best to prioritize your activities
early in the day, before night owls take flight
in pale moonlight, searching for their prey.

The Obligitarians like to spread
their homespun wisdom — everywhere they go:
from city hoods to remote canyon ranches,
from the California coast to the
cornfields of Kansas, offering
their special brand of diplomacy —
allowing each and everyone they meet
to get a word in
edgewise.

Some Poems (No. 4)

Some poems are like pigs in a sty
looking up at the bright morning sky.
Down on the farm there is never alarm
and no one has ever asked why.

FRAGMENTOS

The Owsley Bear lived directly across
from the Denver Zoo,
in order to remain anonymous.

She had painstakingly showed me
the way to her bedroom
only to reveal her fondness for leopards.

Seaside nymphs with luminous skin
splash with delight, in salty resplendence.

God made sperm whales
to go with the humpbacks.

The natives lie naked on the beach.
Mangos!

Tako-kichi!
There must be hundreds of them up there!

The yoke of parenthood must be accepted
before the kids get good and testy.

Apparitions aside, we begin anew.

How many species live in Kalama Zoo?

Remember the four 'R's:
rest, recoup, regenerate, regroup —
then start all over again.

Seeing Is Believing

Winged hedonists move swiftly
around the perimeter, as
church bells ring rather loud.

But this should be of no concern
to the casual observer;
it's up to the formal observer
to report anything unusual.

All's Well On Purdue Mountain

Flies into candle flame
fall into wax and yet remain
true to form.
A singe here and there, but
none the worse for wear,
"A fly wax museum," she says,
succinctly.

Up here, on Purdue Mountain
the fire pit once again
sparks to life. And together
we gather among shadows and stars
where nakedness needs no asylum.

A veil of mist — gently flowing…
fresh herbs on hot bricks — softly glowing…
blue dye and mud formed into Woad,
and placed at five points on faces, smiling.

With wraith-web woven
the silence turns golden, broken
by chanting of words
long forgotten.

With freedom to be
we have gathered good graces,
from season to season
by the moon in its phases.

And all's well on Purdue Mountain,
where the fire pit's soft glow
grows quieter still.
And again we depart to go
our own way —
the way we know best,
only better.

Lakota, I'm With You

I'm thinking about taking a vacation
on the next train to South Dakota
to see if the natives are willing
to construct some kind of pyramid
that will house the ghosts
of massacred Indians
who wander about in search
of their ponies.

And after this great work is done,
standing beneath the late evening sun,
I will lay my weary self down —
and listen to the thunder of buffaloes
winding their way like a wooly wave
across the Golden Plain,
disappearing in a cloud of dust
never to be seen again.

Lakota, I'm with you —
and there's no place I'd rather be,
when the American Dream goes up in smoke
and Crazy Horse comes a calling.

NAVAJO BEAUTY

Catching forty winks
in the back of this bus —
Tucson up ahead, El Paso far behind.
Can it be, Joshua Tree,
by the first light of dawn?

An Indian girl stands and stares
with large brown eyes, her jet-black hair
is tied with red and yellow beads.
And from her ears hang tiny shells
that sway this way and that,
with antelopes dancing on her dress
she gently takes my hat.

I smile in my slumber, knowing all is well,
when Navajo beauty abounds on buses
roaring through dark New Mexico nights.

GLASS MOUNTAINS

Hot rods from hell are near
to where we put an ear
to Glass Mountains.
But this doesn't deter us —
nor dampen our spirits,
since we've placed them safely
in the Spiritual Museum
on West 69ᵗʰ Street, in Cleveland.

We have taken a journey
to study the mysteries:
the magick of alchemy,
the smoothness of stone,
the transparency of light,
the harmonics of sound,
and the aboriginal ambience
only found
in forgotten landscapes
suddenly remembered.

Hot rods from hell — all brightly painted
look scorching in the blazing sun.
Like clockwork, their gears shift;
they fly past us once again,
agitated and reckless, menacing,
like scorpions.

It's a hundred twelve degrees in the desert;
the lizards lie still in the shade.
But we go to where the butte meets the sky
and put an ear to Glass Mountains,
to hear once again the songs of the Earth.

POEM NOIR

At the end of a long, dark hallway
a crack of light beneath a door
serves as a clue to the presence of life
as we know it
at four in the morning.

Slowly, I walk, step by step,
until nearly reaching the door,
I get down on my hands and knees
and put my face to the cool, tiled floor
to take a look and see, staring
right back at me, a solitary eyeball,
dilated, undaunted.

Our gazes transfix and we begin to wink
— simultaneously, rhythmically,
as if we've discovered a new language,
when suddenly the lights go off
and in the darkness, only breathing.

A Side Note

A schematic from another galaxy
transporting itself
through the medium
of consciousness
can appear at any moment
and be seen by many
for unexplained reasons.

FRAGMENTOS

Foghorns could be heard
as far away as Kansas.

A sleeping bear dreams of long ago.

He bared his soul, only to be arrested
for indecent exposure.

Pamela employs the riding crop
when she needs to pick up the pace.

Did Vivaldi ever sleep?

We take a trip down to the Cove,
where flocks of flamingos
and bands of tree frogs
are reconciling their differences.

The unspoken truth speaks for itself.

Waitresses with runners in their stockings
(more flesh than fabric), work frantically
just to keep the lights on.

The best way to keep from getting fat,
is to eat with such intensity that you
burn more calories than you take in.

I'll take geranium over uranium, any day!

No Problem

Dateline: Phoenix: Summer, 2005

The incongruents:
Max Ernst, Man Ray
and Yves Tanguy,
met today
just to see
if posthumously
they could once again
agree to disagree.

It worked!

AN AFTERTHOUGHT

Strung out on subliminals and shoeless —
we wander the streets like transmigrating mutants
searching for signs of an America
we once knew.

For a moment we mingle with marchers for causes,
then turn onto street sales of endless watches —
silverware, hand gloves, and mechanical
cymbal-playing monkeys.

Laughing we go, and you point out to me
relics that remind us of those days long ago —
when dark-skinned ladies of higher consciousness
spoke of revolution in no uncertain terms.

We muse over this and think back to the time
when God was on the lips of everything that moved,
when superfluous details were just swept away,
or scattered in the wind like so many ashes.

WHAT I REALLY MEANT TO SAY

Ambivalent attitudes, unequivocal at times,
continue to ferment in the depths of yet
another consensus resolution.
We take aim, but never strike
the target that is not really a target,
no more a target than
an object of desire that fades
into the background like a wallflower.

What I really meant to say is this:
if a Royal Highness in the bath
is worth two in the bush,
who wouldn't steam up the windows?
And when the handmaidens appear
all decked out in leather —
who wouldn't turn back the clocks?

I don't mean to oversimplify,
but it's your call
when you come out
from beneath the table.

THE EUPHEMISERS

The Euphemisers are down-playing
all serious matters, just to give the air
a chance to clear. In L.A. for example,
the Euphemisers are busy all day and night
and the air is still barely clear enough
to navigate.
Throw in a problem and all hell breaks loose.

Meanwhile, back in New York,
the Euphemisers are doing their best
to put things to rest. They know
that the Big Apple
could use a little peace and quiet,
so they do what they can
which never seems to be enough.

But, one thing's for certain,
the Euphemisers will always
be there when you need them.
For instance, if you're looking for a way
to break some bad news gently,
or to understate a matter of grave concern,
the Euphemisers will gladly offer advice
on how to best soften the blow.

Carousel

The ups and downs of
merry-go-rounds
with tinkling bells and colors
pastels —
await the bright dazzle
at the end of the ride; where
moving sideways
against gravity
satisfied to step
to solid ground,
round and round, we go

like Earth.

Intangibles

Intangibles always change
the composure
of pre-conceived thoughts,
on your way to the grocery store.

Given this: a paradigm shift will often occur
at any given moment, on any given day.

No need to fret.

Intangibles, like vegetables
are not so mysterious when you
consider this: visionaries may be
a dime a dozen, but a cucumber
in the dead of winter
can fetch a buck and a quarter.

Some Poems (No. 5)

Some poems are like peaches and cream
on a hot summer day in July.
When the orchard turns ripe and dripping
with nectar,
Hector will give 'em a try.

Fragmentos

When gardening and bright breasts
signal the arrival of fresh morning rain,
can a bumper crop be far behind?

Just a stone's throw from eternity
and there's no end in sight.

A true mind is a wonderful thing to watch.

Looking through a book entitled,
'Manners for Miscreants'
I notice it has many pages missing.

Philip Lamantia's chanting ape
is most often heard, just before dawn.

If your life is not working — call the hotline.

Dispelling the inner oppressor
gives the liberator some room to work.

Federico Fellini and Italo Calvino
were last seen time-traveling —
in opposite directions.

See you, pseudo or later.

Our love of family is equaled only
by our love of laughter.

Surf Naked

Wet suits are OK, in January —
but what about when
dozens of naked surfers
ride high-cresting waves in July?

What happens when human intelligence
assumes perfect posture —
hanging ten in salty froth?

In this world, some things
were just meant to be...
and the moon turns the tides
for this reason.

WHA?

The old hippies just sat there marveling
at the goings-on around them.
Slow saxophone sounds, blow from the cafe
across the way — as hand drums answer
from the building next door. A fat lady sings
from the window above — something about
the new 'Summer of Love'.
Just then, a car pulls up,
"Is this the suburbs?" asks the driver.
"Oh, no! no! no! — heaven's no!" the hippies exclaim,
shaking their heads and waving their arms in the air.
"Go two blocks and make a left — then go five miles
and take a right — then look for some signs," they said,
assuming the collective voice of authority,
though no one could remember
ever being an authority,
or where the suburbs were for that matter.

CONFETTI

I once knew a young woman
who loved confetti so much
she would often celebrate
for no apparent reason.
Grabbing a bunch in her fist,
with a quick flick of the wrist,
she would send an explosion of color
outside her window
and into the nearest jet stream.

Sometimes she would go through
several bags of the colorful stuff
in just a matter of minutes.
And when asked what she was doing,
she would quickly respond, "don't know,
but don't worry —
it's bio-degradable!"

I Know U R, Butt What M Eye?

Remember way back when you thought
you were minding your own business,
or you were engaged in fair play,
but the next thing you know, you get into a spat
with the boy across the street,
or the girl next door…
And after all the name calling
there was nothing left to say except,
"I'm rubber and you're glue — whatever you say,
bounces off of me and sticks to you!"
Or, "Sticks and stones will break my bones,
but names will never hurt me!"
Remember?
Weren't these early attempts at using a poetic device
to clobber your adversary emotionally?
Well, things have come a long way —
now you can just say, "fuck-off"
and leave it at that.

CRASH COURSE

Back in the days of Higher Learning,
I always kept an eye out for courses
on Eastern philosophy, taking as many
as were offered.
I remember one class when
the professor entered the room,
distributed the syllabus,
gave a brief course description,
then said, "I'd like to begin
by going around the room
and having each of you
say nothing about yourself."
He nodded to me to begin.
Several minutes later, and after much silence,
we were finished.
He dismissed the class after telling us
there would be no reason to return,
we had all passed his final exam.

Material World

Haphazardly we go, with flashers on
wearing raingear
made in sweatshops
by young Ukrainian girls
who go home only to eat and sleep
and dream of the day
when dialectic materials
pre-assemble themselves
leaving them free to journey
to a place where they can dance
the light fandango,
unafraid of any repercussions.

Some Poems (No. 6)

Some poems want to jump off the page
while others will stay in their cage.
So, if you're under a cloud,
for crying out loud,
try smudging the room
with some sage.

Fragmentos

Sacred space: create it, knowingly.

The blue color of sexually excited frogs
is reassuring to students of Orgonomy.

Oh, that darned Ouroboros is at it again!

Long-legged ladies dance through the night,
then search for their shoes by the dawn's
early light.

The sweet tooth is no more.

When Moby Grape took the stage
to open for Country Joe and the Fish —
no one at the time would have guessed
it was the sixties.

A Master of conversational poetry would
look a lot like Gary Snyder.

The electronic wasteland is not so different
than a Salvador Dali painting.

There is great wisdom to be garnered —
once you know where to look.

Joni Mitchell arrived at the studio
for a rendezvous with the blues —
and some new arrangements at her fingertips.

THE PHILOSOPHICAL FAMILY

Talk about transformation!

When driftwood turns into Starwood
the philosophical family gathers on their
porch until it becomes more a platform,
not unlike the ones found at train stations.
And when the engine appears in the distance
there is an excitement, an eager anticipation
that they will soon climb on board.
But the philosophical family doesn't bother
to print up their tickets, preferring instead
to head back inside to see what's cooking.

SMALL TOWN GIRL

What concerns her neighbors
is that she searches for lovers
in all the wrong places.
She thinks what might be going on
inside her head, is some sort of
personality disorder,
but she's really not sure.
So, she goes down to the local drug store
and asks the pharmacist for an opinion
and a large bottle
of an old-fashioned remedy
for a small-town girl
with big city problems.

When she returns home, she opens the bottle
and drinks it down till it's nearly gone.
Just then, there's a knock at the door.
Sure enough, it's Johnny-Come-Lately
wanting to know if she'd like to go for a spin
in his newly souped-up set of wheels.

MANNEQUIN, EH?

She dreamed she was not alone,
and when she awoke she saw
strangers standing all around.
Some were smiling, some were frowning,
some just stared, while others spoke
in hushed tones.
All at once, they asked her
if she was one of them, or just
another mannequin?

Feeling rather piqued by this,
she stuck out her tongue.

ASSEMBLY REQUIRED

A small crowd had gathered to make
some off the cuff remarks
before heading down to meet up
with a larger crowd
that had gathered to
demonstrate their solidarity
in matters concerning their right
to peaceably assemble
by the light of day
or in the dark of night,
for no apparent reason
and for every reason in the world.

A petition of this nature, as a redress
of grievance, will of course require
some crowd control.
Since storm cells will often appear
out of nowhere —
handcuffs and nightsticks
glisten nearby.

LAYLA

Layla said she had lights in her head,
but they were of no help in finding a bed.
So she slept under porches
or in unlocked parked cars,
with her cat in a cage and her bags full of rags,
as if the fundamental meaning of shelter
would be her last refuge.

For Layla whom I met sitting on a curb
at a supermarket parking lot. Elizabeth, NJ. 1972.

FRAGMENTOS

Across a tarnished trash can lid
a caterpillar slowly makes its way.

I never wanted to adhere.

Misconstrued timetables erase the notion
that we can get out of this place anytime soon.

When Eternal Eminence and Ethereal Highness
engage in ecstatic union — a new world is born.

The seed knows.

When spiritual images come to mind
always welcome them in kind.

The spokespeople began speaking all at once.

When you inspire your desire, be sure
to read your expiration date.

No matter when I go to the deli
I always take number 63.

She always wanted to spend more time
at the tip of gravity's slow tongue —
so she took up a weight loss program
and hasn't been seen since.

When you feel like you're getting cold feet,
just turn on the afterburners!

Spoonbill

This is about a play
based on the legend
of a human-like tribe
that possessed spoonbills
and little black tongues.
Once their feathers get plucked,
anything can happen!

Frank Sumatra

Frank Sumatra
stands beneath a banyan tree,
a monkey clinging to his back.
After staring at the ground for a few moments,
he begins to croon softly, tenderly,
reminiscing back to the day
when being a teenage heart-throb
was serious business.

The monkey jumps up on his shoulder
and begins to chatter, showing his teeth
and crossing his eyes.
Frank finishes the song and together
they walk off to the next venue,
on their Indonesian World Tour.

The Cock's Head

Slow beginning — 1
Stern lecture — 2
Swift measure — 3
Slow ending — 1

NIGHT OF SLOW JAZZ

The lips of your lover
are kissing you, and kissing you,
in the darkest night
of slow jazz.
Your love is like a flame,
burning, burning bright —
in the darkest night
of slow jazz.
Soon, you will leave
this world of worry, far, far, behind.
And when you return
the blue notes will sound
much more indigo,
more sanguine, in a way,
leaving you feeling more true
to the moment,
in the darkest night
of slow jazz.

CHECK YOUR TICKETS

Drag queens in limousines
arrive at the Gala affair,
where just the night before
boxers staggered down queer street
asking the referee for directions.
Imagine if you had your nights mixed up!
Wouldn't you be in for a surprise?
Try explaining your way out
of this one —
be it to Beatrice, or to Bruno.

Prisoner Politeness

The prisoners have decided to be polite today,
just to see if it might
melt the bars away. Hey, what the heck,
nothing else had worked, so far.
Now, the guards were caught off-guard by this,
when out in the yard
not a single disturbance did occur.
Not even from Lennie — fucking crazy Lennie.
When other prisoners say you are crazy,
you know you is crazy!
Even crazy Lennie was being cool about it though;
he even tried his hand at being a gentleman,
but fucked it all up.
You know the saying, "it's the thought that counts"?
Well, for Lennie, even an attempt at politeness
was bloc shattering news.
So, at the end of the day, when the bars had
in fact, all melted away —
Lennie walked downtown
and hitched a ride back to L.A.
to take up right where he left off,
before he was so rudely interrupted.

Some Poems (No. 7)

Some poems are like rooms without doors,
some without ceilings or floors,
but once you're inside and there's
no place to hide, you can always
start doing your chores.

Fragmentos

The spokespeople were reassured
that once their tires were inflated,
they'd be ready to roll.

Learn to love, stop being afraid;
kiss the lips that offer you friendship.

Once you resolve to be, for all eternity,
each and every moment
becomes your next to last.

The Rasta Man smiled broadly,
behind compelling dreadlocks.

The day suddenly comes alive —
when Daryl Hannah and Julia Hill
occupy a walnut tree
refusing to come down,
in an attempt to save the City of Angels.

Even if it turns out that there is no God,
it's still fun to imagine it.

Why does Creedence Clearwater Revival always
sound like Huckleberry Finn on acid?

The day comes up, the day goes down
leaving little time for anything else.

"There is a road, no simple highway,
between the dawn and dark of night.
And if you go, no one may follow,
that path is for your steps alone."

—Robert Hunter

ACT III

The Changing of the Mind

Hey, Dude

He rides through the night
in his Bel-Air convertible,
across the dark desert
where the wind blows his hair
and his mind,
loose and wild.
When he arrives at his destination
he will hardly know the place,
but this doesn't concern him.
He knows that in time
everything will click —
just like his fingers
to the tunes on the radio.

One For The Money — Two For The Show — Three To Get Ready — Now, Go Cat, Go!

I made this poem at the end of the day
on my way to bed, weary and worn.
But when it came to me with a few lines
and asked if I cared to elaborate —
how could I refuse?
I said, "Okay" and began to
sketch some words onto paper.
After a few minutes, I paused and asked,
"What would you like your title to be?"
The poem put a finger to its cheek,
gave a thoughtful look and said,
"Let's call me, 'One For The Money —
Two For The Show — Three To Get Ready —
Now, Go Cat, Go!'
"That's not very original," I frowned.
"So what!" screamed the poem,
"call me whatever you like —
but whatever you do,
don't step on my blue suede shoes!"

Pink Chevy To Samahdi

Upon an endless highway, under stars,
roars the pink Chevy —
with chrome and horsepower!
With whitewalls blazing under moonlight —
it flies like a pink flash!

High up on the peaks, above the clouds,
it winds its way. Needing neither
fuel nor driver,
it stops only for hitch-hikers
traveling the high road
and delivers them — often in the wee hours
at the gates of Samahdi.

And it is here, in the first light of dawn
where the pink Chevy shines
in all its glory!

MAE'S DINER

He took the law into his own hands,
clasped tightly, and poof — it was gone!
Just like that, without a trace, without
a whimper or a bang.
Now, you might wonder in a case
like this whether Justice
had rightfully been served.

Well, look no further than Mae's Diner,
where the Justice sits, knife and fork in hand
waiting to be served some meatloaf,
mashed potatoes, and his choice of vegetable,
all due to arrive at any moment.
Once the Justice has been served,
he will begin to look for his just dessert
in another attempt to satisfy his sweet tooth
which of course will never be truly satisfied
at least not to the fullest extent of the law —
nor to a lesser extent, either.

Getting back to our story about this fella
who took the law into his own hands…

When you take the law into your own hands
you better know what you're doing.
This fella happened to know that if he took
the law into his own hands and clasped
tight enough, in just the right way,
he could make it disappear for
as long as it took
to get everything he needed.

An opportunist, you say?
Damn right!

LORETTA

Loretta was pulling his leg
down the sidewalk
leaving a streak of bright blood
which got the attention
of onlookers
out for a Sunday stroll.

Where she was going was
anybody's guess,
but where she was coming from
was quite another matter.

IMAGERY AS POLITICAL DOGMA

According to our cerebral hemispheres
the political images least likely
to be taken lightly, will often lie
left of center, and like a cat
rarely come when called.

The ones most likely to
be overlooked are often found
on the right, and will come on command
like a slobbering hound.

As any political strategist knows,
how quickly you discern the difference
depends upon whose side you're on.

If you're fiercely independent
and wish to remain that way —
you'll stroke the purring pussy at night
and pet the pooch all day.

SOME POEMS (No. 8)

Some poems are clever indeed,
though there's some that you
don't want to feed.
In case you forgot, you can
sweeten the pot, by using the tricks
up your sleeve.

FRAGMENTOS

In Dante Benvenuto's apartment
many years have passed,
and still an unfinished portrait
of George Metesky
peers out from behind bars,
patiently awaiting the final touches.

All for one and one for all
will always co-opt each to his own.

Samsara says, "Your pain is the sum total
of your separation, squared."

When Bob Dylan wrote "Positively 4ᵗʰ Street",
I went there to check it out.

Ask yourself, "Have you been fair,
or have you been foul?"

When you put your mind to it,
the semiotics of Umberto Eco
bring some clarity to disillusionment.

She danced like a hippie at the company picnic.

We can be a wily bunch;
the two of us.

The magic cucumber is indeed charming.

Fifty-Fifty

If more than likely
is just short
of certainty —
and not likely means
a snowball's chance in hell,
what are the odds
you'll make it to the finish line
in one piece?

QUIRK

Cosmic transvestites appear
like little gods in drag
as bitches guard the gates where
blue blooded lesbians hold
snow white monkeys
suckled to their breast.
Breeders in green leotards
look for answers in tarot cards
and finding none
decide to loosen their grip
on conventional wisdom.

No Running Water

Twice a week he would go
down to the river
to take a bath among
the fishes and frogs.
Using soap made of goat's milk
he would sing and scrub,
causing the farmgirls to
whoop and holler!

HARD

It's so hard when I see you
I can hardly walk straight —
my gait a stagger,
my mind awhirl —
but I make my way
to where you are standing
under umbrella,
drizzle falling.

So, what can we say about
short-lived romance?
Your nipples stand firm
beneath your blouse.
And I, too, grow hard
like lost libido, rising
like Lazarus
no longer forgotten.

We stand in silence with
drama unfolding; I take
the umbrella from your hand.
Our arms interlock
and we make our way —
never skipping the chance
to embrace circumstance
and to shake our world
one more time.

SCHRODINGER'S CAT

Stuff comes and goes,
nothing stays —
save the process.
The process stays only because
it goes...

This is a fundamental law of physics:
the formula never leaves a paw-print.

Enduring

It's not about early spring flowers,
or the way she moves
light steps through light years.
She knows only that she is present
and it seems sensible to be so.
From one moment to the next, she
prepares for the day,
dancing through her garden
letting come what may.
She stops to consider some daffodils
before dashing off to ready
herself for the coming millennium.

POLARITY

I think of penguins in their
Polar dimension
Of black and white
Like day and night.
And in the penumbras
Betwixt and between,
They slide on their bellies
Down icy floes.

Fragmentos

Leonora Carrington made her way
to Mexico City,
guided by Angels of Mercy.

Pursed lips leave no doubt.

He kicked in the door of the
Anger Management Classroom —
as a show of solidarity.

If I were Chinese, my name would be Wang So.

Cheap shots rang out, sending the thin-skinned
scurrying for cover.

One unit of awareness is equal
to three moments of pleasure.

Languages are meant to be spoken,
but hearts were not meant to be broken.

When Peckerman's beard points North,
the flight of birds changes course.

Beware the slow drift.

She loved a hairy beast of a man,
for reasons not known to this day.

Sedona took a seat by the side of Oak Creek
and imagined a New Age.

ONE COO BIRD

A dove in the forest sits
quietly watching
and everything she sees
makes perfect sense.
She isn't concerned
with her place in the world;
she and the world are
one in the same.

Voyeur Animalis

Making love on mossy mound
so bright against the green,
what dreams emerge and emanate
like orchids yet unseen.

Beneath the water's misty spray
our auric threads catch light —
and shimmer on this fine, fine day
for in such play our hearts delight.

Fanning the flames of tender tantra,
birds are watching from above
and from below the lizards look
and all around the creatures come

as if by scent, or sight, or sound,
or guided by an inner sense

to witness that mysterious moment
when rapture soars on silver wings
to a world where woodland spirits sing,
leaving us breathless —
a feast for the eyes
of voyeur animalis.

Chancing

"When one chants and dances at the
same time, one is surely chancing."
                    Marilyn Teplitz

Due east of Hades
atop the mound —
it's where the ladies
gather to pound
their drums
and chant
and whirl around
a circle of stone
raising a cone
for brighter days
and darker nights
where fires blaze
for womyn's rites.

For A Green Girl

Conspire to find the prime
lookout spot
in oak-lined
sanctuaries of love,
secluded enough
as in panda bear dreams
yet visible to the eye of newt.

She, being so green,
can hear the plants drinking,
but, then again, hugging trees
whether smooth or craggy
always gave her strength
and a great deal of courage.

She has beautiful ocular orbits
and long slender fingers that
play stringed instruments
for people who have no home.

Some say she was Joan of Arc
several lifetimes ago, though
when asked, she would just laugh
and say, "qu'est-ce que c'est?"
followed by "c'est la vie!"
— which, of course,
only raised suspicions.

Soon, she will find her way
back to the prime lookout spot
in oak-lined
sanctuaries of love,
secluded enough
as in panda bear dreams
yet visible to the eye of newt.

Red Top Tabloids

Through the timelines of tomorrow
she rides upon an ass of sorrow,
with consternation everywhere
and red the color of her hair,
with eyes of blue and skin so fair,
she holds some tabloids to her breast,
upon her bosom they did rest
and as the freaks began to frown
she laid her red top tabloids down.

A schilling here, a six-pence there,
she didn't really seem to care,
what mattered most was on display,
no one could look the other way.
And though the news was hard to take
it never really seemed to break
in such a way to cause a fuss,
or make the old men scream and cuss.
They always welcomed her to town
to lay her red top tabloids down.

ZEBRAS OF THE WILL

Zebras of the Will
file through your door
to munch on tall Serengeti grasses.

It doesn't matter if you're living
in London,
Zebras of the Will
go anywhere.

Perhaps you've seen them
in your own back yard,
or in the hallway of
the building you live in.
Zebras of the Will often congregate
where you least expect to see them.

Franz Kline was influenced by
Zebras of the Will,
and so was Thelonious Monk.
Ebony and ivory are aboriginal in origin…
wide open spaces lie just beyond the pale.

Ringo

At a harmonic convergence, everything
comes together, everywhere at once.
This is what happened to the Beatles
early on, lasting a decade and beyond.

The ley lines of Glastonbury
draw their likeness from Liverpool,
but in a much more diminutive way.
Because of this, melodious sounds are
easily produced and can be heard by those
who are adept at transcribing "ring-tones".
This was known by the ancient Celts
as the magickal practice of *Ringo*
and has nothing to do with the number
of rings on one's fingers.

FRAGMENTOS

The sobs of teenage romantic heartbreak
are often heard when least expected.

Red lipstick, silver glittered face, smiles —
inviting you to try something new.

The trouble is this:
I am both night owl and early bird,
but not necessarily in that order.

Her sudden appearance caused the culprits to flee
leaving their fruit stands unattended.

I remember painting symbols of peace
on enigmatic torsos of bliss.

Hollywood Boulevard is an open-air street museum
for debutantes and derelicts alike.

Hoist me up and cut me loose, Shorty!

The Incredible String Band offered guided tours
into worlds long ago forgotten.

Life is full of mystery, try to imagine it otherwise.

Understand nature and act accordingly.

Easy ape Tuesday at the zoo,
it's where I lay my head and dream of you.

Lot #74

She dresses for the day wearing a
simple lavender dress, identical to
the one she wore the day before.
It's not so much a spiritual thing —
rather a discount
on lot #74.

Yes, My Jesus

When the goddess Eris rises
through the pale vapors of Golgotha,
and her sister Discordia gathers the spoils
and their cousin Kali devours the heads
of fallen angels —
a human manifestation of the divine
appears, nailed upon a cross,
lingering and gathering spiritual momentum
for the final transcendence.

He has known Man before Adam ever knew Eve.
And he has known Woman, before Eve knew
the cat was out of the bag.
And, so, it is said, "in the beginning was the Word"
and He said in the end, "it is finished".

Yes, my Jesus, as you say it:
Love lives beyond flesh.

Blue Goats

Blue goats are with us now,
Ever so young and friendly…
I see you up close in my dreams.
Touching your fingertips
We say hello…
Blue goats are getting restless,
It's nearly time to go.

FOR HER

Sometimes, when the wind blows,
I think of you, and the way your golden curls
cascade down your shoulders.
And when the setting sun turns the sky to pink,
I think about the time you spoke
the language of Venus —
anointing my lips with a water kiss.
Often, I see your smiling face
and the blueness of your eyes
and I remember how silently you stood
in the darkness,
reflecting the silvery beams of the moon.
I thought I saw Sirius in your soul,
but since we have agreed that I cannot see
the forest for the trees,
nor hear the voice that is my own,
how could I be certain of such things?
Yet, watching your hands turn the cards
with magickal intent — the glint in your eye
made me understand why
in those indigo moments, you were
able to skry — so freely.
I remember your song; it was never the same,
but it always sounded like lost enchantment
— to me.
And I will always think dearly of you —
on Lughnasadh,
when His Solar Majesty bid us farewell,
leaving me to wander the night
among the lonely chimeras.

Dolphins

The dolphins come down
from the sky
to their salty domain below.
Then leaping high
with sparkling splendor —
in groups of three
they come and go.

Timewarp

And so we sit in quiet repose,
basking in the afterglow, with red pistachio
stains on our fingers,
wondering how things can be
so complicated —
when we have no use for snakes of sorrow.

Circumstances permitting...
I'll wake you in the morning sun
and barefoot through the sands
we'll go, till we come to a place
where panthers roam
wearing beautiful garlands of roses.
And foxes with faces polished like marble
yawn and show us their tiny red tongues
as strange and funny toads
appear at our feet, quivering
green and golden.

It's not like we've never been here before;
how could we ever forget?

Methinks about the things you said,
about the warping of time
and how rapturous moments
conceive like kind,
as far as the mind can see.

Methinks about how psychic wax
in rivulets will soon define
the measure of our true intent;
who ever said that love is blind?

Beneath candlelight and soft caress
with nothing left to yearn,
we offer up our conjugation
asking nothing in return.

Some Poems (No. 9)

Some poems are like fruit in a bowl,
though that's not necessarily their goal:
some confirm all your fears
others fall on deaf ears,
and some keep the hearts
that they stole.

Fragmentos

Little windows of light bring hope
to the darkened minds of madmen.

Groupies are never as old as the stars.

He tried his hand at archeology, but that didn't work.
So he tried his hand as an auctioneer, only to find
it would leave him in the same predicament as
his neighbor, the yodeling buffoon.

And forgive us our short-comings,
as we forgive those who come up short.

When the milk of human kindness goes sour
— throw it out with the bathwater.

Untoward creatures dive for the shadows.

The fearless ones went running like hell —
their façade being flagrantly violated.

I love the sounds of bongos in the morning.

Q: Who would offer us the Poetry of Fascism?
A: Gabriele D'Annunzio, who else?

Bewildered by everything around him,
he decided to sit snug, not unlike a statue,
yet blinking.

A whirling dervish had to start somewhere.

PLAYHOUSE

Taboos smashed
appear as programs

to plays depicting
lonely housewives

firmly laced
in leather corsets

their libido will loosen
the day's mighty grip.

SWEET DREAMS

My dreams are like veils of silk
sheer on the shoulders of she
who knows me
intimately.
And when they cause her to stir
and draw herself close,
I stroke her cheek with my hand;
though I'm really not there
I can still show I care —
from my hotel room
here in Japan.

LOVEBIRD

Lovebird flies
all brightly feathered —
like a succubus from the netherworld
she illuminates the shadow world,
like an aviator angling through
winds of change: an Empress of the night
looking for her man.

Lovebird makes her nest in my brain
always hatching more of the same.
With panache and plume, she enters the room;
her feathers flutter all around me.

Lovebird knows my beak does not speak,
except in her presence, where it comes unhinged,
that I may sing another day
and we may play another night
in fast and furious flight!

As We Sit

As we sit in the morning sunrise,
I see in your eyes, timeless transcendence
and the true meaning of things.

As we sit in the mid-day sunshine,
I hear in your words, little arpeggios
of affirmation, like sutras set to music.

As we sit in the evening sunset,
I imagine in your dreams, things that
are possible and some which are not.

As we sit in the midnight moonlight,
I feel in your touch, the pristine love
of a heart and mind not withered by time.

And as we sit in this night full of wonder,
I remember you from ages past
when Gaia spoke and we listened.

STAR SPANGLED BETSY

As a salutation,
Star Spangled Betsy
bares her breasts
high atop Mount Rushmore.
It's her way of showing
her gratitude
to the forefathers
carved there in stone.

Try to position yourself
inside her mind's eye,
to see if true patriotism
gives in full measure
the freedom afforded
to one so enamored —
standing right there
on Lincoln's brow.

Balls Of The World

In our study of balls of the world,
we find common threads and we also
find cultural differences that give each
"ball-game" its unique character.

The use of balls in games goes back to ancient times
and has been commonly depicted in petroglyphs,
pottery inscriptions and cave art — right alongside
hunting, copulation and cosmology.

Human fascination with balls most certainly
pre-dates the dawn of civilization and has evolved
into a whole host of ball games played today:

Juggling ball

Baseball	Basketball
Football	Wiffleball
Volleyball	Soccer ball
Dodgeball	Polo ball
Bocce ball	Billiard ball
Croquet ball	Bowling ball
Racquet ball	Squash ball
Lacrosse ball	Tennis ball
Cricket ball	Golf ball
Rugby ball	Soft ball
Pickleball	Pinball
Kickball	Handball

Ping Pong ball

In conclusion, balls of the world have provided
important clues to the evolution of human nature,
particularly regarding the competitive needs of
individuals as well as the cooperative needs of teams.
As we continue to evolve, we can expect new ball games
to emerge for future generations to play and enjoy.

Some Poems (No. 10)

Some poems have vigor and vim —
and some will go out on a limb,
but when push comes to shove
and there's no one to love
you can fill all your cups to the brim.

FRAGMENTOS

Talk to your brain, admonish its indiscretions,
offer it forgiveness, ask only for answers.

The reflection of my shadow puts me
in two places at once.

So how do you portray yourself?

When the calyx of a flower trembles and quakes
you must go quickly to alert the others.

His seafaring skills often left him in the lurch —
so being a Cubs fan, he jumped overboard
and swam all the way to Chicago
in time for the first pitch.

Beelzebub tosses a Molotov cocktail
into the Eighth Bar of Awareness —
where it is quickly consumed by the agnostics.

The rhetorical question is a loaded question,
so be sure to keep the safety on.

Those who dilly-dally, are also known to lollygag.

You cannot circumvent the laws of nature
without consequence.

They're building a new nation across the way.

The Three Franz's

Kafka, Kline, and Liszt
a law firm does not make,
but if you're looking for something
a bit out of the ordinary,
the three Franz's will do just fine.

Supply-Side Economics

It was four o'clock in the morning
and the streets of Philadelphia
were as quiet as they ever get.
Across the way, a homeless man is
standing on a street corner, arms upraised,
shouting over and over, "Help me somebody!
Help me, somebody!
The fox is in the hen house!
Please, somebody, help me!
The fox is in the hen house!"
Now, at first, one would assume
something terrible had just happened,
but this is not the case.
No, he's just one more example
of the down-side
of supply-side economics.

Now You Know

The President is being nonchalant tonight,
going from one wing to the next,
moving the vibes as he goes. He thinks he knows
what's really going on because every morning
they feed him, and then they brief him,
then they send him on his way
to fulfill his obligations
to those who put him there.
Who are "they", anyway?
As far as I know, they are the
'Governmental Circus Agency', the (GCA),
contracted by a secret world order
known as 'Novus Ordo Seclorum'
and they don't want you to know
any of this.

GETTING THE FACTS STRAIGHT

"Facts are stupid things."
           Ronald Reagan

There's nothing quite like getting the facts straight
and placing them at right angles to mere conjecture.
Everyone knows a few facts, like:
Austin is the capital of Texas, or
gravity works only in one direction, or
dogs bark sometimes just to break the silence.

These facts are found in the public domain
and are to be shared freely by all.
Since most facts have no weight to bear,
they can be easily stored in the back of the mind
and brought forth upon request.

Some facts are tried and true, for now and evermore.
Other facts are temporary, and tied to special conditions
making them matters of fact or fiction
depending upon to whom you are speaking.
These are known as elusive facts
and are difficult to nail down,
especially if you find yourself in the dark
more often than you might care to admit.

But, if you'd like to shine some light on this matter,
you can always ask, "is that a fact?"
And if no answer is forthcoming,
you may politely excuse yourself and go
on a fact-finding mission, either alone
or in the company of strangers.

And when you finally do get the facts straight,
having placed them at right angles to mere conjecture,
you can look them over like never before
and marvel at the message they deliver.

WHO DOUBTS PATCHEN?

Returning to this image —

A dog sniffing the face of
a dead soldier.
Hmmm…
did Kenneth Patchen
ever doubt for a moment
that this dead soldier
did not sniff back?
I think not.
Do the dogs of war
ever grow hungry?

Absolutely!

BINGO!

Chance, measured, more or less,
gives happenstance new meaning,
more headroom,
and a chance to win a million bucks
down at the corner drugstore.
Girls playing hopscotch at midnight —
you guessed it…

Bingo!

Why The South Lost The Civil War

It has been said that Jefferson Davis
fled the country after the Civil War,
incognito, dressed as a woman.
Good thing the South lost the war.
Lincoln would never have been able
to pull that one off!

Psycho-patriotic

To those among us, inclined to be
psycho-patriotic, you shouldn't have
to wait a week to buy a firearm.

Deep down South, in Spartanburg, South Carolina,
there's a small garage that does auto repairs.
They do good work at a reasonable rate,
but it takes ten days to get your car back.
The reason it takes ten days for even a minor repair,
is that these mechanics spend most of their time
being psycho-patriotic.

Let's face it, freedom is not something
to be taken for granted.
Life, liberty, and the pursuit of happiness
requires unwavering vigilance.
The enemy has many faces.
You have but one.
You are badly outnumbered.
Just ask any Grandma as she's frisked
and whisked through airport security.

But things could get worse.
What if there were No Enemy?
How would we endure such a lasting peace?
And what would we do with all
the psycho-patriots hiding in the bushes,
armed and waiting?

Thanksgiving Day Prayer

Dear God:
Thank you for these
brief moments of reprieve.
Amen

There's So Many Of You

She entered through the garden gate
and told me that her name was Kate.
I asked her if she'd lost her way;
she told me that she's here to stay.
I asked her if she liked the place;
she told me that her name was Grace.
I asked how many of her there were;
she told me that she liked to purr.
"Fine," I said, "whatever suits."
She asked me if I liked her glutes.
I told her that they looked just fine;
she asked me if she'd crossed the line.
I asked her what did she suppose?
She told me that her name was Rose.

What Is Love?

Men sympathize with men.
Women sympathize with women.
Children sympathize with animals.
Old folks sympathize with everything.
There's plenty of tea and sympathy
Where empathy abounds.

Peace In Our Lifetime

For Linda

Many nights, our two heads
lie in pillows
where silken-spun dreams
reflect like mirrors,
all that we know
and all that we care to know.

Time: like black-veil lace
disappears from your face
and you are young again
like a child
who speaks into the night
about soft sanctuary
where the marmoset play —
in branches beneath skies
full of stars.

I knew you, when pillars were carved
and archetypes sewed their seed.
And I think I will dream about
peace in our lifetime…
where the still waters run deep.
For you are with me, where the
buffalo roam — in this,
our brilliant sleep.

Safety Net

We went to the park to swing
on the swings, but the swings were
no longer there.
The poles held the chains
that swayed in the breeze,
but the wooden seats were missing.

The homeless always need firewood,
and these swing seats were hardly secure,
so their time had come
for a few minutes of warmth
on a cold, snowy day in December.

Looks like we're in for another long winter.

Truth

The truth of the matter is always
Equal to a lie in its conception.
Illusion aside, what matters most
Matters least, until it becomes
Anti-matter.

As a matter of fact, when truth appears
To the naked eye
Wearing tiny raiment of clown clothing,
It's only an attempt
To distract bulls
In rodeos around the world.

To its audience, its beloved,
Truth will always make a curtain call,
As thunderous applause mustered
In amphitheaters
Can be heard in nearby villages.

They say there's never a shortage of truth
When it comes to rude awakenings.
To tell you the truth, the honest truth —
Once the beans get spilled, the
Purveyors of Truth will place them in jars
For those who are not able to tell lies.

WINTER IN STATE COLLEGE

Walking the snow-swept streets
of State College, I imagine myself
as a tour guide
lost on an unknown planet.
Handing out maps of historical markers
and other points of interest,
I take the tour group down to the site where
the legendary Scorpion Bar once stood.
I explain to them how John Lee Hooker
once played here sitting on a stool,
guitar in hand, singing Boogie-Woogie songs
long into the night.
The tour group marveled at this, then asked
if they could make a quick trip to 'The Diner',
in time for a fresh batch of sticky buns.
I relent, with the promise that they congregate
at 6:45, where the My O' My Lounge once
made its mark, and in its hey-day
offered a happening place
for misfits of all persuasions —
joined by truck drivers and topless dancers
for the kind of schooling not offered on campus.

Having finished my reverie, and having dispatched
the tour group, I walk slowly down College Avenue
through the swirling snow.
Arriving at South Burrowes Street, I head for
the big yellow house at the corner of West Foster.
Looking up to a small window on the third floor,
I think of homing pigeons and the important role
they played in their time.

Once inside, with the home fires burning,
I take a seat by the fire and warm my bones.
The events of the day, now tucked away,
and tomorrow come what may
I begin to doze in quiet repose
and listen to the embers crackle and pop.

WHERE CRICKETS GO TO DIE

Why do crickets make such loud noise
on late summer nights and long
into the Fall?
Do they know what lies ahead?
Do they know they'll soon be dead?

What are they saying?
Why, as the days grow shorter
and the nights grow bitter,
do we hear from them less and less?
Soon, there will be only an occasional chirp
until there are none at all.
And in the still of winter's silence,
standing knee deep in fresh fallen snow,
it always seems to beg the question,

where, o' where, did the crickets go?

Printed in the United States
By Bookmasters